I0142224

THIS LITTLE LIGHT OF MINE

By Dominique Redmond

THIS LITTLE LIGHT OF MINE

Published by Lee's Press and Publishing Company
www.LeesPress.net

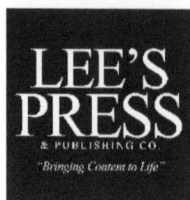

LEE'S
PRESS
& PUBLISHING CO.
"Bringing Content to Life"

All rights reserved, Except for brief excerpts for review purposes, no part of this book may be reproduced or used in any form without written permission from Dominique Redmond and/or the publisher.

This document is published by Lee's Press and Publishing Company located in the United States of America. It is protected by the United States Copyright Act, all applicable state laws and international copyright laws. The information in this document is accurate to the best of the ability of Dominique Redmond at the time of writing. The content of this document is subject to change without notice.

ISBN-13: 978-1732944114 *Paperback*
ISBN-10: 1732944113

DEDICATION

This book is dedicated to my grandmothers Juanita Redmond and Arleta Saxon for being a light to each of their families.

TABLE OF CONTENTS

Dedication i

The Thirtieth Year 1

The Nation is Sleep 2.0 2

Be Quiet 4

View From The Sideline 6

His Cross 8

I am Not Them 10

Putting The Lord First 12

I Had a Baby Boy 13

Soul on Fire 15

Not Yet 17

Their Hearts Have Moved So Far Away 19

Gold 21

Life 22

Thankfulness 24

World On My Shoulders 25

Bodies 27

Water 29

The Past 30

Weather Forecast 31

Home 32

Dinosaur Eggs 34

God's Instrument 37

Gold Shoes 38

Handicap 39

Better 40

Clean Up Crew 41

Fly Above 43

In The Late of the Night 45

Deliverance 47

Tears of a Child 49

R.O.A.R. 51

THE THIRTIETH YEAR

Luke 3:21-23

The Baptism of Jesus

One day when the crowds were being baptized, Jesus himself was baptized. As he was praying, the heavens opened, and the Holy Spirit, in bodily form, descended on him like a dove. And a voice from heaven said, "You are my dearly loved Son, and you bring me great joy."

Jesus was about thirty years old when he began his public ministry.

THE NATION IS SLEEP 2.0

In the last days there will be thunderous times, but yet we stay filled with the intent of self-pleasure. These are the last days, the fiery pits in the ground will open, but even as the earth begins to get destroyed we find new ways of self-pleasure and pleasing our own senses. We have all the signs, we have all the Words, but still in the very last of days we think we have more time to change our lives...to change the lives of others....for that is the true purpose. As spiritual leaders start to fall, what happens when the ones that are called to continue ministry of the nation, called for saving of souls do not answer? What happens when wisdom falls upon deaf ears and insight is reflected upon in hindsight. Ignorance and selfishness are the qualities left in our society. This story is not new, and the past does not only repeat itself but grows deeper. So what becomes of a nation where God is not heard? That is simple...death comes to all, but spiritual life will only come to a few. Do not ignore the urges, the voices, the desires of your heart for WE are called to save the nation of God and carry on his ministry.

Matthew 28:18-20

Jesus came and told his disciples, "I have been given all authority in heaven and on earth. Therefore, go and make disciples of all the nations, baptizing them in the name of the Father and the Son and the Holy Spirit. Teach these new disciples to obey all the commands I have given you. And be sure of this: I am with you always, even to the end of the age."

BE QUIET

Quiet yourself, just listen to me. I will not shout or yell, but I will never lead you to fail. In the days of sorrow or when you are too weak to follow, I say rest for I will carry you further. I never said to take the world on alone or to go in so head strong. In your submission you will receive your deliverance. I have been here watching you tire yourself out, watching you create noise so you could not say you did not listen to me. But we both know you didn't take the time to hear me. I am here and your weight I bear so child sit down and rest and that's when you will be at your best.

Psalm 121

I look up to the mountains—does my help come from there? My help comes from the Lord, who made heaven and earth! He will not let you stumble; the one who watches over you will not slumber. Indeed, he who watches over Israel never slumbers or sleeps. The Lord himself watches over you! The Lord stands beside you as your protective shade. The sun will not harm you by day, nor the moon at night.

The Lord keeps you from all harm and watches over your life. The Lord keeps watch over you as you come and go, both now and forever.

VIEW FROM THE SIDELINE

Sitting on the sideline I have the best view. I learn the moves and also see what not to do. I have become a master at knowing what leads to success, but also what can cause distress. I'm an observer to the game so don't call me in or pass me the ball, for I just came to watch you all.

On the sideline I can watch the show, but don't actually need to be in the know. On the sideline I can talk about the good and the bad, and my two cents I most definitely add. I see the players are getting tired, under constant scrutiny, the game is on-going but I refuse to be subbed in. Is it I am afraid to fail or even worse afraid to prevail? It's safe on the sideline I endure no critism, but at the same time how can we win if I refuse to go in.

On the sideline of Christianity is where I stand. Enjoying my popcorn with Bible in hand. On the sideline living my life too scared, naïve, or proud to play for God's life.

2 Corinthians 6:4-10

In everything we do, we show that we are true ministers of God. We patiently endure troubles and hardships and calamities of every kind. We have been beaten, been put in prison, faced angry mobs, worked to exhaustion, endured sleepless nights, and gone without food. We prove ourselves by our purity, our understanding, our patience, our kindness, by the Holy Spirit within us, and by our sincere love. We faithfully preach the truth. God's power is working in us. We use the weapons of righteousness in the right hand for attack and the left hand for defense.

6

We serve God whether people honor us or despise us, whether they slander us or praise us. We are honest, but they call us impostors. We are ignored, even though we are well known. We live close to death, but we are still alive. We have been beaten, but we have not been killed. Our hearts ache, but we always have joy. We are poor, but we give spiritual riches to others. We own nothing, and yet we have everything.

HIS CROSS

In the middle of it all... the dreams, the failed dreams, the hope and the hope no more. The old and the new, the yesterday's trend, I am the fortress. I am their stronghold. In the middle of Sodom and Gomora I am the refuge for those to come to salvation. My stance is firm, my foundation cannot and will not be moved. In the middle of hell, I bring Heaven. My pillar of hope stands for all to see. Through all darkness the light is still on my "T". I am not happy anywhere else for I call this home. God has created us to withstand so we can be the helping hand. I see God's people falling, I see them prostituting both their bodies and spirit. I see God's people dying. But GOD will be here and HIS Church can and will endure.

Jeremiah 29:11

For I know the plans I have for you," says the Lord. "They are plans for good and not for disaster, to give you a future and a hope.

I AM NOT THEM

Their speech became my speech

Their actions became my actions

Their thoughts became my thoughts

Their harden hearts became my heart

I was sent to enable change as an example, not to judge nor imitate, but surrounded by humanly hate it became innate.

Lord bring me back to the mind and heart of infancy. The place where your pure purpose and spirit reigned in me. On this mission may I continue to know the mind and heart are the greatest to protect. They want my mind and are aiming for my heart, but I have shields the greatest army couldn't imagine. The shields of my life, my purpose no man or human being can touch. My shields, my protection, my faith, will be my strength and carry me on. They may have thought I became them, but with the Lord's focus I am becoming like Him and will increase my power to change the concept of what they consider them.

Romans 12:2

Don't copy the behavior and customs of this world, but let God transform you into a new person by changing the way you think. Then you will learn to know God's will for you, which is good and pleasing and perfect.

PUTTING THE LORD FIRST

Putting the Lord first is for the ultimate joy of self. For when your first joy is in the Lord you are an immovable rock that can withstand any storm. Joy solely in any other person or thing can be like a ship on a wavering sea that goes up and down and can be pulled in a new direction with any unexpected storm. Putting the Lord first will be your stronghold to the path of righteousness.

Matthew 7: 24-27

Anyone who listens to my teaching and follows it is wise, like a person who builds a house on solid rock. Though the rain comes in torrents and the floodwaters rise and the winds beat against that house, it won't collapse because it is built on bedrock. But anyone who hears my teaching and doesn't obey it is foolish, like a person who builds a house on sand. When the rains and floods come and the winds beat against that house, it will collapse with a mighty crash."

I HAD A BABY BOY

Matthew 10:40-42

"Anyone who receives you receives me, and anyone who receives me receives the Father who sent me. If you receive a prophet as one who speaks for God, you will be given the same reward as a prophet. And if you receive righteous people because of their righteousness, you will be given a reward like theirs. And if you give even a cup of cold water to one of the least of my followers, you will surely be rewarded."

I had a baby boy, but I left him in others hands. He had an amazing life, one without strife. I could see him at any time and he welcomed me with open hands to be the parent I should. I chose to visit rarely and I saw him scarcely. Others urged me to, but the days would creep by me and time flew by me. I needed to catch up with friends, to make sure I had material items, to make sure of me others approved.

They brought him to me for others to see, He was 7 then and I hardly knew him. My family was heartbroken as they said I was their key into him. I told them the door was always open and they could go see him anytime. They responded that they would only know him through me, and it was my job to bring them in.

I realized my errors and started building a stronger bond with this now young man, he is almost grown now and will soon go on. He still accepts me with open arms and never associated me with any wrong. I then look back and see the time I wasted on the people I spent time trying to impress. In disgust I recall how my years were spent. Those people tried to change me, change my garments to be dark like theirs and today I finally realized my garments had always been richer than theirs. Not because of money or fabric but because my seamstress created my cloth with a deep foundation.

I had a baby boy who loves me regardless. I need to nurture him, and share his love with others in the world. For I am the key for someone else to access this knowledge, but it's up to me if his love I continue to ignore.

SOUL ON FIRE

There's a fire burning in my soul. I don't know what it is, but it is taking a hold within. I feel it burning deep. My love for Jesus can no longer be contained. I feel it igniting, although I don't know how to expose it. Please let me not resist it but be still. Let me be what you want me to be and set this world ablaze.

2 Timothy 1:6-7

This is why I remind you to fan into flames the spiritual gift God gave you when I laid my hands on you. For God has not given us a spirit of fear and timidity, but of power, love, and self-discipline.

Romans 12:11-13

Never be lazy, but work hard and serve the Lord enthusiastically. Rejoice in our confident hope. Be patient in trouble, and keep on praying. When God's people are in need, be ready to help them. Always be eager to practice hospitality.

NOT YET

I asked to go home and they said "Not yet. We need you to continue, we need you to push through". I told them I was tired, weak. They told me my strength is unlimited and it's my responsibility to spend my energy on the right areas of focus. It is not my duty to know the when, why, or how, but it is my job to take of my being, physically and mentally, so the task placed on me will be completed.

Luke 21:41-46

He walked away, about a stone's throw, and knelt down and prayed, "Father, if you are willing, please take this cup of suffering away from me. Yet I want your will to be done, not mine." Then an angel from heaven appeared and strengthened him. He prayed more fervently, and he was in such agony of spirit that his sweat fell to the ground like great drops of blood.

At last he stood up again and returned to the disciples, only to find them asleep, exhausted from grief. "Why are you sleeping?" he asked them. "Get up and pray, so that you will not give in to temptation."

THEIR HEARTS HAVE MOVED SO FAR AWAY

Their hearts have moved so far away from me

Their actions are blended, their thoughts not solely on me, their songs not solely to me. Their hearts have moved so far away.

Their actions are like mimes, robotic and systematic with no deep emotion nor hint of a smile. Their intentions and gifts are said to be for me, but their hearts has moved so far away from me.

My children of God you cannot serve two Gods. Bitterness, dullness, self-pleasing all takes room in a heart that is meant to serve. Do not let human emotions rob God of the full heart he deserves.

Isaiah 29:13-14

And so the Lord says, "These people say they are mine. They honor me with their lips, but their hearts are far from me. And their worship of me is nothing but man-made rules learned by rote."

GOLD

What benefit is created from a gold miner to find gold and then continue to dig for something deeper. For even if he finds coal he will not know what to do with it. Gold miners understand Gold and a Coal miner understands Coal; when God grants you understanding why ignore the gift of realizations and insight and trade it in for the task of digging for more that is not yet your time to understand.

Psalm 147:5

How great is our Lord! His power is absolute! His understanding is beyond comprehension!

LIFE

Life is like hot running water. Don't waste it!

Psalm 39: 4-7

"Lord, remind me how brief my time on earth will be.

Remind me that my days are numbered—

how fleeting my life is.

You have made my life no longer than the width of my hand.

22

My entire lifetime is just a moment to you;

at best, each of us is but a breath." Interlude

We are merely moving shadows,

and all our busy rushing ends in nothing.

We heap up wealth,

not knowing who will spend it.

And so, Lord, where do I put my hope?

My only hope is in you.

THANKFULNESS

Words cannot explain your beauty, time cannot show your wisdom, eyes cannot handle your greatness. As the sun gleams and radiantly showers on your creations we cannot help but be thankful for all that you do. There is no other greater than you.

I Thessalonians 5:16-18

Always be joyful. Never stop praying. Be thankful in all circumstances, for this is God's will for you who belong to Christ Jesus.

WORLD ON MY SHOULDERS

I had a vision I needed to save the world, so I took it upon my shoulders.

I carried the weight of all mankind's burdens. I decided to be the one to change the world and prepare them for God's word. That's when it crushed me, and I hit the ground in agony; when a soft voice said to me..."I sent a Savior to save the world and He will come again. There were 12 disciples at the last supper all with different purposes and gifts. See I call you all to work together, not for one take over. I call you in peace and In happiness although the road may be treacherous it is never meant for one person's shoulder; so do not give what you do not have for I gave my Son on my behave so you can then apostle on his behalf and a balanced life is what I want you to have."

Romans 12:5

So it is with Christ's body. We are many parts of one body, and we all belong to each other.

BODIES

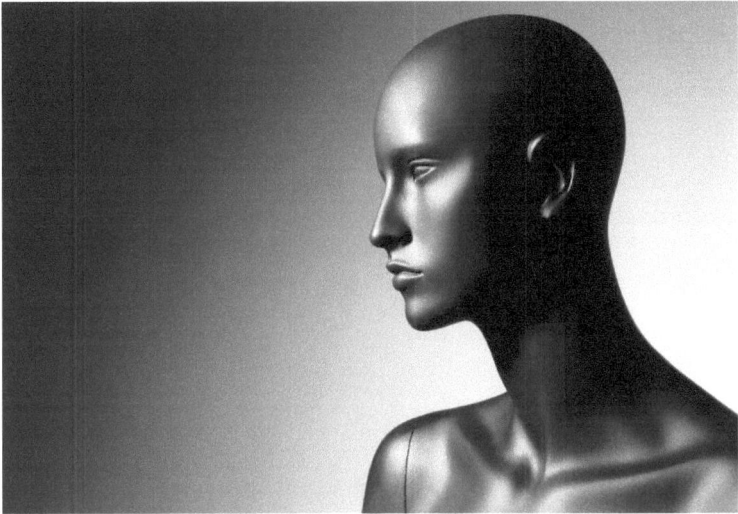

Bodies, bodies, we need to move bodies. What's the count of bodies? Bodies that walk emotionless, that fall in line and follow the shamelessness. What's the count of bodies? Get ready. Your turn is next, to degrade yourself, throw out your morals, use your body as enticement, flaunt your gifts as vulgarity, use your vessel to speak profanity. Bodies, bodies, what's the count of bodies? We need more they say, so come in line. It is easy to not think for yourself, we will show you just what to do. For under another's control you don't need a mind...we just want your body.

Among the recruiters you can be one of the best of them all. They will follow your moves and do what you do. You will be their leader and learn how to influence the masses. But underneath the motions your conscience is still there. For in a second you pause and realize how many bodies you have moved. Moved toward hate, moved toward deceit, moved toward gossip, moved toward death. They are not you, you say but a remembrance of each body stays with you so that the weight of guilt is weighing you down. Snap back…you don't care they are just bodies, you are moving bodies. But in your heart when you know wrong from right, when you have the power of influence to do what is right if you choose to move bodies toward wrong or even sit back and watch as they go…then consider your body…where do you go?

The power is there, and power is making a choice. To continue to move bodies to destruction or to speak and offer instruction. Non-action is an action, so by non-movement we create a movement. A movement of allowing them to move bodies. From fear of saying what is right? From fear of their might? But on that night when we face the ultimate might and HE really moves bodies. Do you want there to be silence on your regard? Or do you want to at least be able to say…"I tried to make them do right"? The power of influence is not only a sin when used for destruction, but is an injustice when we fail to give correct instruction.

Romans 12:1

And so, dear brothers and sisters, I plead with you to give your bodies to God because of all he has done for you. Let them be a living and holy sacrifice—the kind he will find acceptable. This is truly the way to worship him.

28

WATER

1 Peter 3:21

And that water is a picture of baptism, which now saves you, not by removing dirt from your body, but as a response to God from a clean conscience. It is effective because of the resurrection of Jesus Christ.

I was lost. So I went seeking for myself. When I got there, there were scary unknown faces so I took a detour to the water. It was safe and welcoming, where I could leave all my troubles, hassles, and worries. In the water they all were so free. In the water the calmness of grace took over. I was lost so I went on a journey to find me, but in my searching the Lord found me. Stop working so hard to create the image of what you want. Leave your worries and get in the water, for then you can see what it is that the Lord should have you to be.

THE PAST

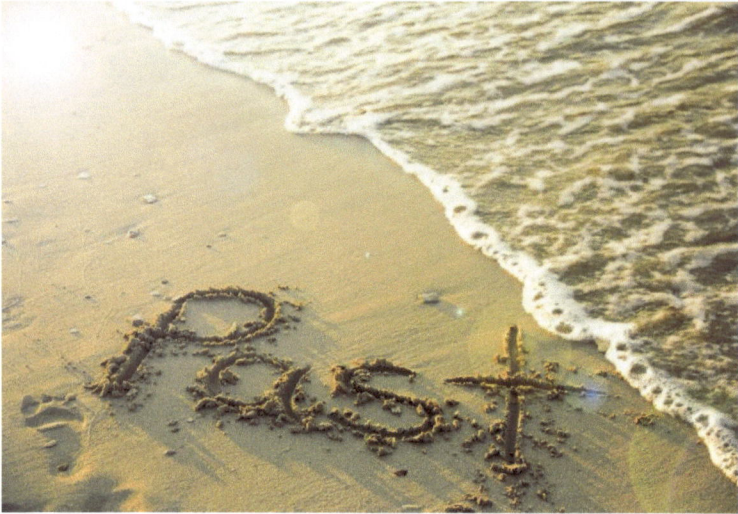

When I asked about the past they told me they were all dead. I asked them what happened and they each had their own story. Different paths each took, different decisions made, but no one was sad because it was in the past.

Philippians 3:12-14

I don't mean to say that I have already achieved these things or that I have already reached perfection. But I press on to possess that perfection for which Christ Jesus first possessed me. No, dear brothers and sisters, I have not achieved it, but I focus on this one thing: Forgetting the past and looking forward to what lies ahead, press on to reach the end of the race and receive the heavenly prize for which God, through Christ Jesus, is calling us.

WEATHER FORECAST

Grey skies in the forecast but my sun is still shining. Doctors predict grey skies in the forecast but my skies are still bright. My job shows rain storms for the day but my life is still with dry weather. My relationship has thunderous storms, but my God, my sun is still shining. For not through me but through thee is my destiny and my weather prediction. The winds can throw at me what they may, but the Lord predicts sunshine on this day.

Philippians 4:6-9

Don't worry about anything; instead, pray about everything. Tell God what you need, and thank him for all he has done. Then you will experience God's peace, which exceeds anything we can understand. His peace will guard your hearts and minds as you live in Christ Jesus.

And now, dear brothers and sisters, one final thing. Fix your thoughts on what is true, and honorable, and right, and pure, and lovely, and admirable. Think about things that are excellent and worthy of praise. Keep putting into practice all you learned and received from me—everything you heard from me and saw me doing. Then the God of peace will be with you.

HOME

I went home today. I left the pain for an hour and a half, I
went home. I sat with my Father and He consoled me. I sat
with my Father, He held me. He reminded me where I
came from, and what I experience is a mere fragment of
time compared to the eternity I have and will spend with
Him. He reminded me of my pure joy, my power, my
purpose. For all things are possible for those that believe. I
went home today, and my Father reminded me the door is
always open, but it's my choice to enter it. Home restored
my soul. Home restored my heart. Home restored my joy.
Home reassured my Faith. When is the last time you went
home?

Psalms 145:13-19

For your kingdom is an everlasting kingdom. You rule throughout all generations. The Lord always keeps his promises; he is gracious in all he does. The Lord helps the fallen and lifts those bent beneath their loads. The eyes of all look to you in hope; you give them their food as they need it. When you open your hand, you satisfy the hunger and thirst of every living thing. The Lord is righteous in everything he does; he is filled with kindness. The Lord is close to all who call on him, yes, to all who call on him in truth. He grants the desires of those who fear him; he hears their cries for help and rescues them.

DINOSAUR EGGS

This is an old building, built before my time. This old building is where many secrets lie. Hurt, trouble, problems, lies, monsters all tucked in this old building. Some have been here since the beginning and know each secret these walls hold, but ignoring them is easier then acknowledging them for with acknowledgment comes responsibility so silence is the remedy.

New blood comes and sees a mystery, Dinosaur eggs blocking the pathways to streams. Streams of growth, streams of truth, streams of God. They are not hard to see, but also easy to ignore.

Dinosaur eggs old as ancient times, no one knows exactly who laid them and no one ask where they came from. Without learning the history how do we solve this mystery?

Dinosaur eggs are blocking the pathways, but who will take on this journey of discovery? Dinosaur eggs represent the old, which no one speaks of. The boulders that created road blocks, the hurt feelings from a wrong doing, the lies that caused hearts to hardened. These dinosaur eggs are as old as time but the damage is still shown on prime time. Dinosaur eggs so large no one man can conquer, but without addressing the history of their creation how can we move forward in any situation.

When asked only some chose to speak about it. The eggs have been there and at times people have tried to remove them and the building had life, but again and again the eggs appear and create a blockage and strife. A stranger asked to those that would speak "well why don't they address the beast that plant the eggs so that there is final defeat?" They turn and walkaway because no one wants to be assigned that task.

Puzzlement and confusion sets in the strangers eyes, how be so complacent when living among lies. There are dinosaur eggs here blocking spiritual growth but yet the town walks around like no one knows. They celebrate and live for this old building but who is contributing to the building. Such passion and faith is a cover for fear and hate. Dinosaur eggs as old as time are in this old building and that is where the problem lies. A cycle that will be everlasting because people continue to turn and walk away as no one wants to be assigned true discovery. Unless you conquer the source of blockage from the root it will eventually conquer the building at the root. For these Dinosaurs eggs that have existed since ancient times will cause the building to fall and you will see the final destruction of all.

Haggai 1:4-5; 7-9

"Why are you living in luxurious houses while my house lies in ruins?" You have planted much but harvest little. You eat but are not satisfied. You drink but are still thirsty. You put on clothes but cannot keep warm. Your wages disappear as though you were putting them in pockets filled with holes!...This is what the Lord of Heaven's Armies says: Look at what's happening to you! Now go up into the hills, bring down timber, and rebuild my house. Then I will take pleasure in it and be honored, says the Lord. You hoped for rich harvests, but they were poor. And when you brought your harvest home, I blew it away. Why? Because my house lies in ruins, says the Lord of Heaven's Armies, while all of you are busy building your own fine houses.

GOD'S INSTRUMENT

I am a tool, an instrument of God. I could not work until I let go, I could not produce meaningful outcomes until I stopped trying, I could not make a difference until I realized it wasn't my difference to make. The difference God makes… in my life, in your life, in the world, when we release power and allow ourselves to be used. I am a tool, an instrument of God.

2 Timothy 2:20-21

In a wealthy home some utensils are made of gold and silver, and some are made of wood and clay. The expensive utensils are used for special occasions, and the cheap ones are for everyday use. If you keep yourself pure, you will be a special utensil for honorable use. Your life will be clean, and you will be ready for the Master to use you for every good work.

GOLD SHOES

My shoes are bedazzled with jewels and made of the finest fabric imaginable. They gleam in the light and shine so bright throughout any night.

Her shoes have flare, another pair glides across the floor gleaming. The gold shoes fit each of us differently, and we each tailor them to fit our individual originality. Each of us has a pair of gold shoes that the world should see, all presented differently, but all great. Showcase your gifts and slip on your gold shoes for the world to see.

1 Corinthians 12:4-7

There are different kinds of spiritual gifts, but the same Spirit is the source of them all. There are different kinds of service, but we serve the same Lord. God works in different ways, but it is the same God who does the work in all of us.

A spiritual gift is given to each of us so we can help each other.

HANDICAP

You are getting a new pair of legs, so get up and walk. You have been in the wheelchair long enough and accepted life as we must. You are getting a new pair of legs now so now get up and walk. The shock and disbelief that miracles can happen are keeping you stagnant. Your legs are waiting, so will you get up and walk?

Matthew 17 :20-21

"You don't have enough faith," Jesus told them. "I tell you the truth, if you had faith even as small as a mustard seed, you could say to this mountain, 'Move from here to there,' and it would move. Nothing would be impossible."

BETTER

It gets better…that's what I always knew. The struggle doesn't last forever, that was a constant reminder. The storm was for a reason, is what repeated in my head. Long days, weary nights, it does get better. Keep your head high, your faith strong, for what is revealed to you in a storm may be what you need to feel better. Endure the rain for we all need it to grow, and even when your better you might find that you enjoy different seasons. It will always get better and remember no matter what the Lord is there in all weather.

Job 42:12

So the Lord blessed Job in the second half of his life even more than in the beginning. For now he had 14,000 sheep, 6,000 camels, 1,000 teams of oxen, and 1,000 female donkeys.

CLEAN UP CREW

After a storm there is a clean-up crew. They clear the trash, decide what is salvageable and decide what to throw away. Life is the same, we sometimes need to be our own cleanup crew. Different things about ourselves and about others. We need to take these & re-organize instead of trying to put them all back to where they once were. Trash does not always mean you throw it away, but sometimes you let go & let God have His way. In life let's not hoard onto the past, but let the clean-up crew of God re-organize our path.

Psalm 51:10-12

Create in me a clean heart, O God.

Renew a loyal spirit within me.

Do not banish me from your presence,

and don't take your Holy Spirit from me.

Restore to me the joy of your salvation,

and make me willing to obey you.

FLY ABOVE

The pain, the hurt, the judgement, the ridicule, the nay Sayers, the hypocrites, the negative energy. Fly above yourself to see life from the Ariel view. The view too great for man to comprehend, but the view that brings peace on earth. That everlasting view that is deliverance, the view that only faith can help you rise to, the view where no tear shall fall and no condemnation is involved, the view from the wings of Angels.

Psalm 91:9-16

If you make the Lord your refuge, if you make the Most High your shelter, no evil will conquer you; no plague will come near your home. For he will order his angels to protect you wherever you go.

They will hold you up with their hands so you won't even hurt your foot on a stone.

You will trample upon lions and cobras; you will crush fierce lions and serpents under your feet!

The Lord says, "I will rescue those who love me. I will protect those who trust in my name. When they call on me, I will answer; I will be with them in trouble. I will rescue and honor them. I will reward them with a long life and give them my salvation."

Isaiah 40:31

But those who trust in the Lord will find new strength.

They will soar high on wings like eagles.

They will run and not grow weary.

They will walk and not faint.

IN THE LATE OF THE NIGHT

In the late of the night when my mind is at rest that is when the devil is at his best. My thoughts, my fears, my tears he comes to conquer them all. In the late of the night that's when my Angels fight. Scriptures. Faith. Prayer. Those are my shield. In my weakness comes the enemy, but in the faithful he has no victory. Prepare yourself for the war that happens in the late of the night. Amen to the Most High for in the morning comes new light. Hope reassured, joy, and a new chance to achieve our purpose. Don't let the time periods of our life that equal the late of the night define our life. All things are possible to those that believe!

Psalm 91:1-8

Those who live in the shelter of the Most High will find rest in the shadow of the Almighty. This I declare about the Lord: He alone is my refuge, my place of safety; he is my God, and I trust him. For he will rescue you from every trap and protect you from deadly disease. He will cover you with his feathers. He will shelter you with his wings. His faithful promises are your armor and protection. Do not be afraid of the terrors of the night, nor the arrow that flies in the day. Do not dread the disease that stalks in darkness, nor the disaster that strikes at midday. Though a thousand fall at your side, though ten thousand are dying around you, these evils will not touch you. Just open your eyes, and see how the wicked are punished.

1 Peter 5:8-11

Stay alert! Watch out for your great enemy, the devil. He prowls around like a roaring lion, looking for someone to devour. Stand firm against him, and be strong in your faith. Remember that your family of believers all over the world is going through the same kind of suffering you are.

In his kindness God called you to share in his eternal glory by means of Christ Jesus. So after you have suffered a little while, he will restore, support, and strengthen you, and he will place you on a firm foundation. All power to him forever! Amen

DELIVERANCE

Deliver me from my own mind so that my whole heart can be focused on you. Deliver me from my own wants so that my actions are in your alignment. Deliver me from my own tongue so that the words I speak are pleasing to you. Deliver me from this selfish heart that puts me before HE.

Psalm 19:12-14

How can I know all the sins lurking in my heart?

Cleanse me from these hidden faults.

Keep your servant from deliberate sins!

Don't let them control me.

Then I will be free of guilt

47

and innocent of great sin.
May the words of my mouth
and the meditation of my heart
be pleasing to you,
O Lord, my rock and my redeemer.

TEARS OF A CHILD

The tears of a child, there are none. For the pain of life is every day, what we call misery is their reality. How do you describe happiness when it has never been experienced? No tears will fall for sorrow is what they call normal. Tears of a child will never be seen for death, rape, and abuse is what became okay. Jesus says let the children come to me, but how do we help these lost sheep? They seem too far gone, there are too many and where to begin? The answer is simple and the effort is easy. The call is to be there. No person can change what atrocities have happened but one loving hug, conversation, gesture can penetrate a hardened heart that can break through the stone and eventually allow love to be shown. The tears will never fall and a smile may never show, but to be there may make the difference that you never know.

Matthew 9:36-38

When he saw the crowds, he had compassion on them because they were confused and helpless, like sheep without a shepherd. He said to his disciples, "The harvest is great, but the workers are few. So pray to the Lord who is in charge of the harvest; ask him to send more workers into his fields."

Mark 10:13-16

One day some parents brought their children to Jesus so he could touch and bless them. But the disciples scolded the parents for bothering him.

When Jesus saw what was happening, he was angry with his disciples. He said to them, "Let the children come to me. Don't stop them! For the Kingdom of God belongs to those who are like these children. I tell you the truth, anyone who doesn't receive the Kingdom of God like a child will never enter it." Then he took the children in his arms and placed his hands on their heads and blessed them.

R.O.A.R

I used to have dreams & wanted to take over the world. I was going to run my life and with no plan I went for it.

It was more work than I thought. The disappointment of people, experiences, and life overall slowly chipped away at my eager energy.

The once enthusiastic Tiger inside became exhausted; a trapped animal at the zoo who ran out of energy to escape. Now they are opening the doors, but what is the use? His prime is over, he is not a young cub anymore, he has seen so much in his time that he does not care to explore more.

Resting…laying…that is how he remains. For what is the use as he knows the work ahead. As much as he longed to be free, the zoo is now where he is choosing to be. He can see all he wanted right before his eyes, but his legs are too weary and his heart is not as passionate. He closes his eye; a tear falls down his golden fur. Is this the life you wanted? No, but it's the life I accepted. This could be the end, but deep in his soul he knows he has more. All the regret, all of the pain, all of the friends & family that are not present anymore, he takes it with him as these form the knowledge that is helping him grow.

As he rises and slowly walks he tries to ignite the passion of the young cub, but sometimes it is difficult. He sees the road ahead and just gets exhausted, but he knows more things now. He sees a stream ahead, but knows it's a trap of men, for he has seen fellow tigers get captured there. He moves along slowly gaining momentum. He struts…he walks briskly…he starts to gallop…he starts to run…he starts to ROAR. For in his spirit he feels the rush. For every hardship & lesson that knocked him down has made him the strong person he is today. He didn't achieve his dreams when he thought he should, but as a cub he had ambition & no knowledge. Now it is not easy to restart the flame, but he is trying & has much to gain. It would be easy to lie on the zoo floor & accept what life had become, but the hardships created him to be much more. He was captured like so many & convinced this was the end, but GOD lived in him and said our journey has just begun.

I am GOD I know all things. I know you are tired, I know you are lost, I know you are scared. Don't lay there defeated for you hear my voice. Rather in your heart, in nature, in a song, from a person, you hear my call for you, don't ignore it. Only you know what is right for you. I will give you the will to go on. Don't just lie there. I know it's hard, but I need you to go on & do the will of GOD...

I NEED YOU TO ROAR!

R.O.A.R. Realizing Our Ambition & making it Reality

2 Corinthians 4:16-18

That is why we never give up. Though our bodies are dying, our spirits are being renewed every day. For our present troubles are small and won't last very long. Yet they produce for us a glory that vastly outweighs them and will last forever! So we don't look at the troubles we can see now; rather, we fix our gaze on things that cannot be seen. For the things we see now will soon be gone, but the things we cannot see will last forever.

www.ingramcontent.com/pod-product-compliance
Lightning Source LLC
LaVergne TN
LVHW010021070426
835508LV00001B/1